GCSE English Language
Revise Description Writing
Model Answers and Practice
from
GCSEEnglish.uk

Edward Mooney

gcseenglish.uk

Copyright © 2023 by Edward Mooney

All rights reserved. This book or any portion thereof may not be reproduced or used in any manner whatsoever without the express written permission of the publisher except for the use of brief quotations in a book review or scholarly journal.

First Printing: 2023

ISBN 979-8512087695

www.gcseenglish.uk

Contents

Introduction	1
1: A journey by bus	3
2: A description of an old person	7
3: A description of a marketplace	11
4: A description of a beautiful place	15
5: A description of a mysterious place	19
6: A description of a familiar yet unusual place	23
7: A description of the sky	27
8: A description of the day after a festival	31
9: A description of a shop	35
10: A description with the title 'Downhill'	39
11: A description of a crowded street	43
12: A description of a factory	47
Appendix 1: Exam Board Information	51
Appendix 2: What the examiners are looking for	52

Introduction

In this book, you will find the guidance you need to help you improve your description writing.

There are practice exam-style writing tasks, writing checklists and complete full-marks model answers to help show you what a good answer looks like and what the examiners are looking for.

The descriptions are short – no more than 750 words – and show what is achievable within the constraints of a timed exam.

Description writing is a very important part of the English curriculum and is assessed at GCSE, representing up to 25% of your total GCSE grade, depending on your exam board. Regular practice of description writing is therefore vital for boosting exam grades.

Regular description writing practice will also help boost your confidence in other forms of writing.

How to use this book

There are a range of different ways you can use this book. You could:

- read the descriptions and see what an excellent exam answer looks like.
- read the exam tasks and then plan and write your own descriptions.
- use the checklists (provided after every description) to see how many of the writing recommendations are met by each description.
- use the checklists (provided after every description) to help you plan and write your own descriptions.
- read the descriptions again, more slowly, identifying key language features (e.g. imagery, simile, metaphor, personification).

Of course, these are practice tasks and model answers. Your writing in your exam should be your own work. Don't attempt to memorise a description and copy it out as you risk being penalised, such as having marks taken away or even being disqualified from the entire exam.

More about me

I am a qualified teacher of English with a degree in English Literature from the University of Cambridge. I have taught and examined GCSE and A Level English courses at outstanding schools since 2006. I now write model answers and provide exam preparation through my website gcseenglish.uk.

Keep up to date with future projects and collections of model answers by subscribing to my newsletter or by following my social media channels. Visit gcseenglish.uk or search gcseenglishuk and feel free to leave a review.

Best of luck in your exams!

1: A journey by bus

You are advised to spend the correct amount of time on this section (check Appendix 1 for your exam board's time).
Write in full sentences.
You are reminded of the need to plan your answer.
You should leave enough time to check your work at the end.

You are going to enter a creative writing competition.

Your entry will be judged by a panel of people of your own age.

Describe a journey by bus as suggested by this picture:

Photo by Melanie Brown (@itsmelb) on Unsplash.

1: The Description

The bus eases up to the kerb and stops with a hiss and a sigh. The doors flap open and the scrum of waiting passengers, faces grey and empty after a long day in the city, shuffles forward, eager to get out of the unforgiving November rain, to get home. Nervous eyes scan along the length of the bus, noting how full it already is. Some, at the back of the scrum, have already given up, resigned to waiting for the next one, their escape from the city delayed.

The doors swing shut, and the bus pulls away into the night. The rear lights twinkle and refract in the driving rain. They gleam red, and are gone.

The rammed bus picks up speed as the driver skips a few stops. A shiver of hope passes through the crowd – home early tonight.

Each lurch of the vehicle, each bump, pothole, sleeping policeman, humpback bridge, each clunk of clutch and gear, sends the passengers' heads swaying in harmony, like wheat buffeted by a strong summer gale.

Then there's a shout and the bus screeches to a stop, toppling the standing passengers like skittles. The driver makes her feelings known in rather brusque language to the motorcyclist who, she argues, had the temerity to cut her up. The passengers right themselves, checking for blood and bruises, rolling their eyes and wishing for home.

But the incident has broken the vow of silence and now the passengers start chatting away.

"No need for that, was there?"

There is a hum of agreement.

"Honestly, she gets worse every day."

The journey drags on. A nurse, weak with fatigue, is falling asleep, her head against the window. The vibrating and juddering do not wake her. It's been a long shift.

A coffee shop worker, barista of the year, is reading. In the novel, earnest people lead powerfully meaningful lives in exciting locations. By contrast, from the bus window can be seen: roundabouts, traffic cones, prefab light industrial buildings, derelict railway sidings, boarded up shops. The barista turns the page, preferring the balmy beaches and exquisite glamour of the fantasy world of the story.

The bus reaches the dual carriageway. Not far to go now. There are fields out there, somewhere in the darkness.

An old man, in a black suit almost as old as him, is lost in thought. The tie is black too and between his hands he holds an order of service. He looks down at the face on the front of the pamphlet, a photo taken in younger days of a man proud and happy, before the illness got to him. Another one gone. The man sighs. He measures out his life by funerals now, by bad sandwiches and muted conversations with grieving widows.

The rain is still beating down as the bus pulls into the market square and stops. The end of the line.

The final passengers walk across the slippery cobbles and disperse into the tiny lanes and alleys that lead off into the dark. Above them soar the two towers of the old church, floodlights picking out the buttery yellow of the ancient stone.

Unimpressed, the bus heads back to the city, ready to go again.

1: Writing Checklist

As you read, check how many of the recommendations below are followed by the description. Then, use the checklist to help you write your own.

Remember that these are *recommendations* from an experienced teacher, not *requirements*. Allow them to help and guide you, but don't allow them to restrict you; if you have a different idea and feel confident and excited about it, then give it a go!

- ☐ Create an emotional 'journey'.
- ☐ Structure by passing of time and/or by shifts in focus.
- ☐ Describe time of year and day.
- ☐ Describe weather.
- ☐ Describe colours.
- ☐ Describe sounds.
- ☐ Describe tastes, smells and touch sensations.
- ☐ Describe people.
- ☐ Describe/suggest their emotions.
- ☐ Use a small amount of direct speech.
- ☐ Use symbolism.
- ☐ Zoom in to tiny details.
- ☐ Zoom out to bird's-eye view.
- ☐ Speed pace up/slow pace down.
- ☐ Freeze time.
- ☐ Use present tense.
- ☐ Describe the past of the scene.
- ☐ Describe the future of the scene.
- ☐ Use imagery, simile, metaphor, personification.
- ☐ Use paragraphs and sentences of varied length.
- ☐ Use accurate spelling, punctuation and grammar.
- ☐ Write c450-c750 words.

2: A description of an old person

You are advised to spend the correct amount of time on this section (check Appendix 1 for your exam board's time).
Write in full sentences.
You are reminded of the need to plan your answer.
You should leave enough time to check your work at the end.

You are going to enter a creative writing competition.

Your entry will be judged by a panel of people of your own age.

Write a description of an old person as suggested by this picture:

Photo by Balazs Kovacs on Shutterstock.

2: The Description

The eyes, nut-brown and speckled like a bird's wing, gaze out, beyond, through and past; it never ends, it seems, this gaze that has seen so much and lived so long. For he is old, this man, and these eyes have seen billions of images flutter and flit before them. He stands now, quietly running his hand through his beard, ruminating, contemplating, gathering those memories, the warp and weft of a life well-lived, trying to grasp, one last time, what it all meant.

On his knee is a scar, a pale ghost of the gaping wound it commemorates, a memorial to the day he met with triumph and disaster in the course of five minutes of play for the Silfield under 11s. Every time he retells the story, another detail is added: a mazy dribble, a Cruyff turn, a dummy, a one-two off his best mate and the slick swoosh of the ball slotting into the top corner. Then, the twist, the crack and the scream as the defender came at him studs up. The end of a promising career.

His hands, heavy and thick, flesh scored and scarred by decades of labour, hang limply now, their work done. Each crack in his skin tells a story of a load of glistening asphalt, flowing and oozing, spread with care on motorways the length and breadth of the land. His shoulders ache, a permanent reminder of rammers and drills and all manner of diesel hungry tools. He still has his high-vis and work boots, just in case there's another cutting, tunnel or culvert to dig.

The beard is wiry silver now but in the right sunlight a chestnut sheen can still be detected, an echo of what was once a vivid red, like the tail of a fox. Red too was the mewling, scrunched up face of the new-born he once held gingerly in his arms. Red too were the tulips he proudly grew in the garden of the house he bought, red brick of course, for his new family. He parked the red Cortina in the drive and for a while life was good.

He knows, though, that life can save up cruel surprises for the unsuspecting. He struggles to walk now and needs to lean, out of breath, on a walking frame as once he leant on his shovel. It was the asbestos that got to him. He coughs now and blood flecks mark his hankie. Yet he lives. He survives. At the hospital, they nod as he passes. This is his life now.

Those nut-brown eyes gaze down at a forest of tubes and wires. His face creases with pain and sadness.

"Can you hear me Mary?" he says, hoping for the flutter of an eyelid, the quiver of a lip. "I'm here again today." He takes her hand. "It's rainy out. You're sensible to be indoors where it's nice and warm."

Soon, he knows, he will be looking down into the cold earth of her grave but for now, his eyes look past the drips and the hissing ventilator to see her and to see the life they had together.

The eyes will be alone soon. But not yet.

2: Writing Checklist

As you read, check how many of the recommendations below are followed by the description. Then, use the checklist to help you write your own.

Remember that these are *recommendations* from an experienced teacher, not *requirements*. Allow them to help and guide you, but don't allow them to restrict you; if you have a different idea and feel confident and excited about it, then give it a go!

- [ ] Create an emotional 'journey'.
- [ ] Structure by passing of time and/or by shifts in focus.
- [ ] Describe time of year and day.
- [ ] Describe weather.
- [ ] Describe colours.
- [ ] Describe sounds.
- [ ] Describe tastes, smells and touch sensations.
- [ ] Describe people.
- [ ] Describe/suggest their emotions.
- [ ] Use a small amount of direct speech.
- [ ] Use symbolism.
- [ ] Zoom in to tiny details.
- [ ] Zoom out to bird's-eye view.
- [ ] Speed pace up/slow pace down.
- [ ] Freeze time.
- [ ] Use present tense.
- [ ] Describe the past of the scene.
- [ ] Describe the future of the scene.
- [ ] Use imagery, simile, metaphor, personification.
- [ ] Use paragraphs and sentences of varied length.
- [ ] Use accurate spelling, punctuation and grammar.
- [ ] Write c450-c750 words.

3: A description of a marketplace

You are advised to spend the correct amount of time on this section (check Appendix 1 for your exam board's time).
Write in full sentences.
You are reminded of the need to plan your answer.
You should leave enough time to check your work at the end.

You are going to enter a creative writing competition.

Your entry will be judged by a panel of people of your own age.

Describe a marketplace as suggested by this picture:

Photo by Ja Ma (@ja_ma) on Unsplash.

3: The Description

The first hardy souls are here long before sunrise. On cold winter mornings, under the sodium glow of the streetlights, a ragtag fleet of transit vans pulls into the market square, tyres squelching on damp cobbles. A fox, disturbed from his nightly ramblings, slinks off back into the darkness. With efficiency born of years on the road, a tangle of poles and brackets, trestles and awnings, is transformed into a vibrant trading hub, ready to bring the world to this small Norfolk town.

There is a pause. The horizon brightens. The market traders are always first in the nation to see the sun, out here in the East. They sip dark tea from thermoses, stamp their feet, exchange pleasantries. They brace themselves. They are ready.

The first customers come for the fish. The fishmonger calls out the prices and the daily catch from behind a wall of blue ice boxes. Hidden among the crushed ice are rivers of silver, smudges of pale pink and folds of deep white. Plucked from the profound cold of the North Sea only yesterday, by this evening they will be on the menu at a local restaurant, *á la meunière*. The last box is emptied and all that remains is a scatter of ice shards and rainbow scales, that catch the light from the risen sun.

Time for breakfast and the tea and bacon sarnie stalls are doing a roaring trade as workers and school students pass through the market on their way to the daily grind. The grills sizzle and hiss. The bottle of brown sauce is upended and thwacked. Eggs are cracked, fried and slapped onto buttered bread in moments. Coffee machines work at the double, providing the sharp deep caffeine jolt that kick-starts the day.

"Get your five a day! Finest Norfolk bananas! Fresh from the leafy Norwich banana groves!" Passers by laugh at the patter, shivering under the cold winter sun. Here are the greengrocer's wares: punnets of winter strawberries, bringing a splash of summer to the frosty day; apples piled high, the forty shades of green; orange swedes as big as your head, still carrying clods of damp earth; cabbages that would make good footballs; and hessian sacks of golden spuds. We'll eat well tonight.

For tonight is coming. The sun dips early in midwinter and now the temperature is dropping. The streetlights flicker on, first pale red then strengthening to Lucozade orange. The market traders slip the last shiny pound coins into their money belt, take a look around and call it a day. Time for home and a hot bath. Time to sit down for the first time all day.

The awnings come down, the trestles are collapsed, and the stalls are packed away. The fleet of vans slips away into the gloom and the market square falls silent.

The fox returns and prowls again across the market square. He sniffs, stands alert, then moves. There on the cobbles lies a punnet, half squashed, that somehow missed the sweeper's broom. He crouches and feasts on bulging hothouse strawberries, glad of sugar in the depths of winter.

3: Writing Checklist

As you read, check how many of the recommendations below are followed by the description. Then, use the checklist to help you write your own.

Remember that these are *recommendations* from an experienced teacher, not *requirements*. Allow them to help and guide you, but don't allow them to restrict you; if you have a different idea and feel confident and excited about it, then give it a go!

- ☐ Create an emotional 'journey'.
- ☐ Structure by passing of time and/or by shifts in focus.
- ☐ Describe time of year and day.
- ☐ Describe weather.
- ☐ Describe colours.
- ☐ Describe sounds.
- ☐ Describe tastes, smells and touch sensations.
- ☐ Describe people.
- ☐ Describe/suggest their emotions.
- ☐ Use a small amount of direct speech.
- ☐ Use symbolism.
- ☐ Zoom in to tiny details.
- ☐ Zoom out to bird's-eye view.
- ☐ Speed pace up/slow pace down.
- ☐ Freeze time.
- ☐ Use present tense.
- ☐ Describe the past of the scene.
- ☐ Describe the future of the scene.
- ☐ Use imagery, simile, metaphor, personification.
- ☐ Use paragraphs and sentences of varied length.
- ☐ Use accurate spelling, punctuation and grammar.
- ☐ Write c450-c750 words.

4: A description of a beautiful place

You are advised to spend the correct amount of time on this section (check Appendix 1 for your exam board's time).
Write in full sentences.
You are reminded of the need to plan your answer.
You should leave enough time to check your work at the end.

You are going to enter a creative writing competition.

Your entry will be judged by a panel of people of your own age.

Describe a place you think is beautiful.

4: The Description

Now, all places have their beauty, especially the ones overlooked by advertisers and social media influencers. Even an oozing fen, exhaling pungently, clogged with half sunken boats, with the towering chimneys of a sugar beet factory dominating the horizon, is as majestic as the Alps or the Taj Mahal, and easier to get to. Or perhaps the tangled derricks and cranes of a working dock with a rainbow sheen across the still water as a vast tanker arrives from Vera Cruz, blotting out the sun as it eases into its berth. Here is beauty too.

A midsummer day, high in the chalk hills that sweep down to the sea, is when I find beauty. It takes some effort though. Behind the school runs a bridleway, choked with nettles and the occasional fly-tipped mattress. Blackthorn bushes grasp and grab with murderous intent, their thorns long enough to penetrate to the heart. Ahead though, beyond the murky darkness is a patch of bright light, signalling hope and the open hillside.

I explode out of the maelstrom of stunted trees, stinging leaves and spiny hedges, glad to be free of their grasp, into the glorious sunlight of summer and the joyful laughing song of soaring larks. The path is now a shimmering streak of chalk, reaching out to the summit. As I walk, butterflies, lazily taking the sun on the warmed path, rise up for a moment in an explosion of colour and then flutter down behind me, back to sleep.

I stride along the path. The larks keep singing.

Great bulbs of flint lie cracked among the chalk, revealing their dark glistening hearts to the sun. Verdant wooded valleys open out to the north. To the south, all along the bend of the coast, the sea shimmers. A cyclist approaches at speed in a cloud of white dust, eyes intent on the path ahead, fingers feathering the brakes, a trickle of sweat falling from her brow. I step aside and watch her fly.

Almost to the summit and now there are brown cows, gazing at me lazily, grazing and ruminating as I pass. There are ponies too, cropping at the grass, whisking their tails at the insects that buzz and gather and swoop. Flaming yellow furze bushes fill the air with coconut fragrance.

The larks keep singing.

Now I head into the labyrinth of ditches and banks that encircle the hill. For this is not any old hill. Thousands of years ago, the first people to climb this hill came here looking for flint. They dug deep into the chalk using hand tools and launched a stone age revolution. I tread gingerly across the hilltop, threading my way between collapsed mine shafts, now overgrown and loud with bees.

A concrete pillar marks the summit. Climb to the top, spread your arms wide, let the sun bathe your face, and turn to gaze over this green and pleasant land. Look far to the south, you may see the golden beaches of Normandy.

The larks are singing still. They float and glide, higher still and higher, carefree spirits of a beautiful place.

4: Writing Checklist

As you read, check how many of the recommendations below are followed by the description. Then, use the checklist to help you write your own.

Remember that these are *recommendations* from an experienced teacher, not *requirements*. Allow them to help and guide you, but don't allow them to restrict you; if you have a different idea and feel confident and excited about it, then give it a go!

- [ ] Create an emotional 'journey'.
- [ ] Structure by passing of time and/or by shifts in focus.
- [ ] Describe time of year and day.
- [ ] Describe weather.
- [ ] Describe colours.
- [ ] Describe sounds.
- [ ] Describe tastes, smells and touch sensations.
- [ ] Describe people.
- [ ] Describe/suggest their emotions.
- [ ] Use a small amount of direct speech.
- [ ] Use symbolism.
- [ ] Zoom in to tiny details.
- [ ] Zoom out to bird's-eye view.
- [ ] Speed pace up/slow pace down.
- [ ] Freeze time.
- [ ] Use present tense.
- [ ] Describe the past of the scene.
- [ ] Describe the future of the scene.
- [ ] Use imagery, simile, metaphor, personification.
- [ ] Use paragraphs and sentences of varied length.
- [ ] Use accurate spelling, punctuation and grammar.
- [ ] Write c450-c750 words.

5: A description of a mysterious place

You are advised to spend the correct amount of time on this section (check Appendix 1 for your exam board's time).
Write in full sentences.
You are reminded of the need to plan your answer.
You should leave enough time to check your work at the end.

You are going to enter a creative writing competition.

Your entry will be judged by a panel of people of your own age.

Write a description of a mysterious place, as suggested by this picture:

Photo by Kyle Mackie (@macrz) on Unsplash.

5: The Description

Thousands of people must walk past it every day, this crumbling archway of knapped flint that huddles out of sight, quivering on the edge of vision, there but not quite there. Commuters, school children, shoppers, joggers – all of them speed down the wide boulevard, never casting their eyes to the left. It's not their time to take this journey. Not yet.

One November night, cold and glittering with frost, when the full moon fills the street with a buttery lake of light, a grieving insomniac soul slips unnoticed down the alley and pauses before the arch. "All hope abandon", inscribed across the curve of the arch, keeps the nervous out but this traveller shrugs. Hope died for him long ago.

It's time to take the journey. He plunges into the beyond.

Music dances in fragrant summer air, tracing jigs and reels in notes that gambol across the sky. The cares of winter slip away as the shadow of the arch falls behind. Meadow flowers turn the world Technicolor and the monochrome world of winter fades into memory.

There is someone ahead, treading lightly along a chalk path. He carries an accordion slung across his back. Then there are others carrying fiddles and whistles and twelve-string guitars. The traveller looks around and sees; he is not alone.

"Welcome," they say as they pass by. "It's a long time we've been waiting for you."

Briars bend in obligingly, offering their dark fruit. The traveller tastes the mellow sweetness of the best of summers. A stream runs close by the path. He bends and drink its life-giving coolness, silver and sparkling, the water of life.

There is a town ahead and the crowds thicken along the way, as everyone seems to be going to the same place. Domes and spires, towers and turrets pierce the sky and on the edge of town, running down to a mighty river, is a grassy meadow where marquees, trestles, merry-go-rounds and dodgems are ready for the great summer fair.

All faces are eager now as crowds gather on the meadow, ready for the party to start. The local mayor, resplendent in a tricorn hat, golden chain shimmering under the noonday sun, declares the festivities open and pipers strike up a happy tune. The old man with the accordion joins in, puffing and panting as he pushes and pulls the ancient bellows. Whistles and fiddles toot and scrape and old songs are sung to the strumming of guitars.

And the food! Warm bread straight from the oven, thick slices of blue cheese, sharp slivers of onion. Great vats of soup bubble merrily away. Bowls of summer fruit and generous pours of rich cream. Glasses of the first apple cordial of the year are swigged freely.

Lost in the revels, the traveller doesn't notice the old woman sitting quietly on a straw bale, gazing happily at the antics of the party goers. But later, stumbling laughing off a rollercoaster, he catches sight of her, pauses for a moment, then heads for a glass of cordial, then turns back. He recognises her then and a cold shiver passes through his whole body. He remembers the day he said his last goodbye to her: the cawing ravens, the lone piper, the sprig of honeysuckle dropped into the open grave.

The music and laughter fades into background noise as he approaches and asks her with her eyes if it's true.

She nods. It is her and she reaches to take his hand.

"Welcome," she says. "Welcome my child. It's a long time I've been waiting for you."

He stumbles to earth and closes his eyes. What is this place?

5: Writing Checklist

As you read, check how many of the recommendations below are followed by the description. Then, use the checklist to help you write your own.

Remember that these are *recommendations* from an experienced teacher, not *requirements*. Allow them to help and guide you, but don't allow them to restrict you; if you have a different idea and feel confident and excited about it, then give it a go!

- [ ] Create an emotional 'journey'.
- [ ] Structure by passing of time and/or by shifts in focus.
- [ ] Describe time of year and day.
- [ ] Describe weather.
- [ ] Describe colours.
- [ ] Describe sounds.
- [ ] Describe tastes, smells and touch sensations.
- [ ] Describe people.
- [ ] Describe/suggest their emotions.
- [ ] Use a small amount of direct speech.
- [ ] Use symbolism.
- [ ] Zoom in to tiny details.
- [ ] Zoom out to bird's-eye view.
- [ ] Speed pace up/slow pace down.
- [ ] Freeze time.
- [ ] Use present tense.
- [ ] Describe the past of the scene.
- [ ] Describe the future of the scene.
- [ ] Use imagery, simile, metaphor, personification.
- [ ] Use paragraphs and sentences of varied length.
- [ ] Use accurate spelling, punctuation and grammar.
- [ ] Write c450-c750 words.

6: A description of a familiar yet unusual place

You are advised to spend the correct amount of time on this section (check Appendix 1 for your exam board's time).
Write in full sentences.
You are reminded of the need to plan your answer.
You should leave enough time to check your work at the end.

You are going to enter a creative writing competition.

Your entry will be judged by a panel of people of your own age.

Describe a familiar place at an unusual time or from a different point of view.

6: The Description

This shouldn't be possible. The ring road, normally clogged and heaving at this time of day, is silent. The air above, so often hazy and speckled with soot particles, is clear and fresh as an Alpine meadow. I pedal, dazed, along the centre of the dual carriageway and realise, as I slow to give way when reaching a roundabout, that I'm still following the Highway Code.

So, I pedal hard and zoom across the middle of the roundabout, through the little grove of trees at its centre, and burst out the other side. I ignore the No Entry sign and speed down the hill towards the marketplace. Still there is no one. The city is mine.

Is that what the Vikings saw, the day their longboat first slid upriver and moored in the marshy land down by the cathedral? A city abandoned in sheer terror. Panic and oppressive silence. Trembling fear about what's to come.

The market stalls are all boarded up. The gathered detritus of the last moments before the panic fills the alleys: fish and chips wrappers, the last edition of the evening paper, a punnet of raspberries. Signs of haste and fear are everywhere. Out on the high street, cars sit where they were abandoned. A seagull eyes me lazily from the roof of a van before launching into the air with a cry.

I head for the supermarket, crunching on shattered glass. Inside, the perishable foods are long gone. A rat scurries by me, annoyed at being disturbed from its scavenging. But that is exactly what I'm up to. I head for the tins though not many are left. I load up on dented un-labelled cans, glad of any food. Even if it's sardines and custard for dinner tonight, my hungry body will welcome the calories. And so will my family.

I hear a noise and scarper. Staying in one place for too long is not a good idea.

The sun is declining but before I make a dash for home I head for the castle. It looms over the city as it has done for a thousand years and for the last few years, it's been my place of work. I cycle up the spiral path that encircles the motte, puffing as I reach the top. The yellow stone glows in the evening sun. I look out over the city and see the familiar skyscape and hear the unfamiliar, oppressive silence. The buses that would usually be passing by around the bottom of the motte stand idle. The little park that would normally be full of children, screaming and laughing on the monkey bars and slides, is empty of course.

I feel the cold of the key in my hand and open the castle door, bracing for the alarm that doesn't sound. Inside, the exhibits huddle unseen, not that they were ever very popular. The dark quiet of the museum isn't new. Landscapes by minor local painters, eighteenth century ballgowns, portraits of long forgotten textile merchants and Lord Mayors lie in wait in the crepuscular gloom.

I know what I'm looking for. I move quickly through the castle to the main exhibition and there it is, unmistakeable even in the gloom as it still glows, a dull, beautiful yellow, bringing light to the darkness. I remember watching people's reactions to it as they came through the exhibition. Eyes glistened, faces lit up. Viking gold. Pillaged no doubt, ill gotten, then inscribed with mysterious runes and lost, buried for centuries. There is something so glorious about it. People can't help but stop and stare.

And now it's mine. I speed home and my family greet me at the door, relieved to have me back again. I can see the hunger and the fear in their eyes. I feel the heavy weight of the gold in my pocket and silently thank the Viking who buried it. A little insurance for whatever happens next.

6: Writing Checklist

As you read, check how many of the recommendations below are followed by the description. Then, use the checklist to help you write your own.

Remember that these are *recommendations* from an experienced teacher, not *requirements*. Allow them to help and guide you, but don't allow them to restrict you; if you have a different idea and feel confident and excited about it, then give it a go!

- ☐ Create an emotional 'journey'.
- ☐ Structure by passing of time and/or by shifts in focus.
- ☐ Describe time of year and day.
- ☐ Describe weather.
- ☐ Describe colours.
- ☐ Describe sounds.
- ☐ Describe tastes, smells and touch sensations.
- ☐ Describe people.
- ☐ Describe/suggest their emotions.
- ☐ Use a small amount of direct speech.
- ☐ Use symbolism.
- ☐ Zoom in to tiny details.
- ☐ Zoom out to bird's-eye view.
- ☐ Speed pace up/slow pace down.
- ☐ Freeze time.
- ☐ Use present tense.
- ☐ Describe the past of the scene.
- ☐ Describe the future of the scene.
- ☐ Use imagery, simile, metaphor, personification.
- ☐ Use paragraphs and sentences of varied length.
- ☐ Use accurate spelling, punctuation and grammar.
- ☐ Write c450-c750 words.

7: A description of the sky

You are advised to spend the correct amount of time on this section (check Appendix 1 for your exam board's time).
Write in full sentences.
You are reminded of the need to plan your answer.
You should leave enough time to check your work at the end.

You are going to enter a creative writing competition.

Your entry will be judged by a panel of people of your own age.

Describe what you see, hear and feel when you look up into the sky as day changes into night.

7: The Description

The great disc of the sun, the boiling cauldron of fury and energy, bringer of fire, crucible of life, is drawing near to the end of its daily journey. Night is coming. Yet, the sun is reaching also the end of a different journey, its long migration north bringing the gift of summer, for today is the solstice. I reach the hilltop, settle down into soft bracken and lean back on the standing stone that guards the summit, feeling the bluestone coolness on my back, rooting me to the earth. I send my gaze aloft. The landscape hushes.

The greatest show in the universe is about to start.

Out to the west, the sun plunges into the sea in an explosion of colour. Reds and oranges, livid streaks, splash the sky and ring clouds with a golden halo. The sea, mirror calm, is molten flowing silver, slowly cooling to a soft dull gleam. The last birds of day rise to sing their valediction, the playful notes falling from the air, joy with a mourning cadence. Bees buzzing among yellow furze blossom sip their last drops of nectar and head home to the hive, the day's work done. I breathe in the cool, perfumed air of evening and feel the strains and pressures of the day take flight and disappear, out into the darkling sky, out into the cold forbidding universe.

I turn my gaze to the east, whence the darkness comes. The sky dissolves into the blues and indigoes of night and the clouds, delicate puffs of vapour soaring high in the stratosphere, now seem a deep black. Behind them, peeping at first, nervous in the wings, then stepping out proudly onto the stage, are the real stars of the performance – the constellations and galaxies and streams of ancient light, pin prick fossils of long dead supernovae, from furthest space but gathering in pleasing patterns to guide, teach and entertain the people below. There's the swan, spreading vast wings in a protective embrace. There's the eagle, gliding high above us all, eyes clear, all-seeing. And there's the North Star, ever fixed, a guide for the wandering ships that pass silently on the sea below.

The broad arm of the Milky Way now rises, spiralling across the heavens in an elegant dance to the music of the spheres.

I feel at home in the vastness of it all.

The night is short and soon the first birds pip and chirrup and warble their chorus of joy and welcome, launching themselves high into the sky as the darkness fades to grey. The world is monochrome for a moment as the stars fade. Then, imperceptibly at first, and then, it seems, in a refreshing, overwhelming flood, colour returns to the world. An arc of blue in the east and the splash of yellow on the furze bushes. I stand to greet the sun. Our old friend explodes from the far horizon, fire and life again, boiling gold. The sky is cloudless. It's going to be a hot day, but I am shivering.

I head home through fields of ripening grain. The cold dew hangs heavy on the wheat, harbinger of the seasons to come.

The earth has tilted. Today is summer, but winter is coming.

7: Writing Checklist

As you read, check how many of the recommendations below are followed by the description. Then, use the checklist to help you write your own.

Remember that these are *recommendations* from an experienced teacher, not *requirements*. Allow them to help and guide you, but don't allow them to restrict you; if you have a different idea and feel confident and excited about it, then give it a go!

- [ ] Create an emotional 'journey'.
- [ ] Structure by passing of time and/or by shifts in focus.
- [ ] Describe time of year and day.
- [ ] Describe weather.
- [ ] Describe colours.
- [ ] Describe sounds.
- [ ] Describe tastes, smells and touch sensations.
- [ ] Describe people.
- [ ] Describe/suggest their emotions.
- [ ] Use a small amount of direct speech.
- [ ] Use symbolism.
- [ ] Zoom in to tiny details.
- [ ] Zoom out to bird's-eye view.
- [ ] Speed pace up/slow pace down.
- [ ] Freeze time.
- [ ] Use present tense.
- [ ] Describe the past of the scene.
- [ ] Describe the future of the scene.
- [ ] Use imagery, simile, metaphor, personification.
- [ ] Use paragraphs and sentences of varied length.
- [ ] Use accurate spelling, punctuation and grammar.
- [ ] Write c450-c750 words.

8: A description of the day after a festival

You are advised to spend the correct amount of time on this section (check Appendix 1 for your exam board's time).
Write in full sentences.
You are reminded of the need to plan your answer.
You should leave enough time to check your work at the end.

You are going to enter a creative writing competition.

Your entry will be judged by a panel of people of your own age.

Write a description with the title, 'The day after the festival'.

8: The Description

The weather broke at just the right time. The final chords had been played, the last pints of cider had been poured and the final sky lantern had been released, sweeping up into the darkness, before being engulfed by the thunder cloud that had been billowing, looming, mutating all afternoon above the heads of the festival goers. The awesome cumulonimbus tore itself asunder, sending the stragglers running for shelter, flooding tents, collapsing marquees and creating rivers of mud out of hard midsummer earth.

Dawn reveals post-apocalyptic devastation. Bleary-eyed revellers crawl in shock from their tents, mud-smeared and dazed, trudging through town to the railway station, desperate for home and bed. The station buffet can't keep up with demand for bacon sandwiches and mugs of tea. Shocked commuters flinch away from the muddy hordes, hoping not to ruin their suits. Each train departs crammed to the roof. The guard, used to a quieter morning shift, gives up on checking tickets and retreats to the vestibule, waiting for the storm to pass.

Back in the town square, a familiar face can be seen at a hotel window. Down in the marketplace, his fans shout and wave, their patience rewarded. They break into the chorus of his latest hit. The frontman offers his blessing to his adoring followers, miming along with their singing, before retreating back into the sanctuary of the hotel room. The fans, ecstatic to have seen their idol, keep singing.

Down by the river, its usual pacific trickle now swollen and angry after the night's deluge, cars lie at crazy angles half submerged in mud. A raven and a dove swoop overhead. Frustrated revellers, tired and hungry, push desperately on the boots of cars as engines gun and mud splatters high into the air. Wellies lie discarded, stuck deep in the earth as their owners shrug and wander the field in socks. Then, a convoy of tractors arrives to cheers and soon the field is cleared. The farmers save the day.

The clean-up continues as an army of high vis descends on the site. Miles of wiring are retrieved, spooled onto giant spindles and transported to the next festival site. Festoon lights are removed from the hawthorn hedges and the field is starting to look itself again. The portaloos are hoisted onto flatbed lorries and driven off at haste. Rubbish bags pile up for collection. Suddenly, there is a cry, and someone emerges, yawning and stretching, from a half-crushed tent. They gaze around in surprise. Where is everyone? A passing clean-up volunteer laughs and gives them a slap on the back; there's always one that misses the train.

Now the field falls silent as peace comes dropping slow into the lazy heat of the midsummer afternoon. A sheep wanders through the devastation, nibbling at a few remaining blades of grass and the townspeople breathe a sigh of relief as the storm abates. Time to celebrate, time to count the money and then time to prepare for next year. The raven and the dove soar high again over the festival site and a rainbow glimmers in the clouds.

8: Writing Checklist

As you read, check how many of the recommendations below are followed by the description. Then, use the checklist to help you write your own.

Remember that these are *recommendations* from an experienced teacher, not *requirements*. Allow them to help and guide you, but don't allow them to restrict you; if you have a different idea and feel confident and excited about it, then give it a go!

- [ ] Create an emotional 'journey'.
- [ ] Structure by passing of time and/or by shifts in focus.
- [ ] Describe time of year and day.
- [ ] Describe weather.
- [ ] Describe colours.
- [ ] Describe sounds.
- [ ] Describe tastes, smells and touch sensations.
- [ ] Describe people.
- [ ] Describe/suggest their emotions.
- [ ] Use a small amount of direct speech.
- [ ] Use symbolism.
- [ ] Zoom in to tiny details.
- [ ] Zoom out to bird's-eye view.
- [ ] Speed pace up/slow pace down.
- [ ] Freeze time.
- [ ] Use present tense.
- [ ] Describe the past of the scene.
- [ ] Describe the future of the scene.
- [ ] Use imagery, simile, metaphor, personification.
- [ ] Use paragraphs and sentences of varied length.
- [ ] Use accurate spelling, punctuation and grammar.
- [ ] Write c450-c750 words.

9: A description of a shop

You are advised to spend the correct amount of time on this section (check Appendix 1 for your exam board's time).
Write in full sentences.
You are reminded of the need to plan your answer.
You should leave enough time to check your work at the end.

You are going to enter a creative writing competition.

Your entry will be judged by a panel of people of your own age.

Imagine you work in a shop. Describe a time when the shop is particularly busy.

9: The Description

The queue is already out the door as the afternoon shift arrive for work. They dump their bags in the staffroom, pull on faded uniforms and laminated name badges and head for the shopfloor, annoyed to have drawn the short straw. The morning shift scarper, casting apologetic glances at their colleagues; they are glad to be off on this of all afternoons.

The checkout operators take their places and look out over the unprecedented scenes before them. Each aisle is crammed with customers, grabbing and reaching, filling baskets and trolleys to the brim, pushing past each other, ducking under outstretched arms. Shelves are emptying quicker than the shelf stackers can keep them filled. The operators exchange glances, apprehensive.

"It's like the pandemic all over again."

They start to work, scanning, packing, swiping. They get into a rhythm, a trance, moving quickly. The beeping sounds like 1970s electronica, the music of an imagined future.

The crowd swells as more people squeeze into the shop. Many are wearing the yellow and green of the local football team. Yellow and green ribbons tie back hair from excited faces. Some have painted their entire faces, one half yellow, one half green. They probably regret it now as the sun beats down and the paint smears and drips from their chins. Every now and then, one of them breaks into song:

"Top of the league, having a laugh!!"

"Going up, up, up!!"

The shift manager, who also drew the short straw, checks her watch. Kick off is soon. They just have to get through the next few hours.

Sausages are in high demand – it's barbecue weather after all. Burgers are snapped up. Red peppers, cheese, baps, condiments, onions, are flying out of the shop. Colman's mustard, yellow, spiky, aggressive, is a particular favourite. Some of the more confident shoppers buy champagne to celebrate victory, hoping to toast the team's health after the final whistle.

A camera crew rolls up outside and a local news reporter starts doing a piece to camera.

"I am here in the city centre where hopes are high, and fans are preparing for the party to end all parties."

Cars zoom past, scarves waving out the window, horns blaring. The queue is starting to dissipate.

Back inside, shoppers nervously check their watches. Some, scared of missing kick off, abandon their trolleys and slink away. The barbecue can wait, it seems. The match takes precedence. As the minute hand ticks towards three o'clock, an eerie silence falls and the stunned checkout operators look up, rubbing their eyes and stretching. They've never seen the shop like this. Outside, the roads fall silent. The whole city is on edge.

The shift manager puts the kettle on and tells everyone to have a well-deserved break. She tunes in to the match and they sit and listen to the commentary which echoes from the ceiling in the empty shop. Soon, the hordes will return, either in ecstasy or in grief but for now they rest and wait, willing the team to victory.

9: Writing Checklist

As you read, check how many of the recommendations below are followed by the description. Then, use the checklist to help you write your own.

Remember that these are *recommendations* from an experienced teacher, not *requirements*. Allow them to help and guide you, but don't allow them to restrict you; if you have a different idea and feel confident and excited about it, then give it a go!

- ☐ Create an emotional 'journey'.
- ☐ Structure by passing of time and/or by shifts in focus.
- ☐ Describe time of year and day.
- ☐ Describe weather.
- ☐ Describe colours.
- ☐ Describe sounds.
- ☐ Describe tastes, smells and touch sensations.
- ☐ Describe people.
- ☐ Describe/suggest their emotions.
- ☐ Use a small amount of direct speech.
- ☐ Use symbolism.
- ☐ Zoom in to tiny details.
- ☐ Zoom out to bird's-eye view.
- ☐ Speed pace up/slow pace down.
- ☐ Freeze time.
- ☐ Use present tense.
- ☐ Describe the past of the scene.
- ☐ Describe the future of the scene.
- ☐ Use imagery, simile, metaphor, personification.
- ☐ Use paragraphs and sentences of varied length.
- ☐ Use accurate spelling, punctuation and grammar.
- ☐ Write c450-c750 words.

10: A description with the title 'Downhill'

You are advised to spend the correct amount of time on this section (check Appendix 1 for your exam board's time).
Write in full sentences.
You are reminded of the need to plan your answer.
You should leave enough time to check your work at the end.

You are going to enter a creative writing competition.

Your entry will be judged by a panel of people of your own age.

Write a description with the title, 'Downhill'.

10: The Description

From the trig point, the whole nation is laid out before us, a patchwork quilt of fields and farms, peaks and valleys, counties and cities. A three hundred and sixty degree turn around the mountain top reveals it all, shimmering far below. Joy, excitement and adrenalin fill our hearts. Smiling, we take photos for posterity.

A snow bunting pips and chirrups, hopping among the stones scattered across the summit. There is snow here, a remnant, a whisper, of the harsh storms of winter that scour the summit. Under the July sun, the snow now drips and trickles, ice crystals glittering, soon to disappear in the dog days of summer.

A raven, strong and quiet, perches on a rock, gazing down into the chasms below.

Tea cheers us and readies us for the descent. With one last look out over the country and one last photo, we head downhill. The path is busy as we are not the only fools who enjoy the pain of hiking up into the sky. Some pause for breath, faces red, hands on knees. Others collapse onto the stones and vow never to do anything like this again. Among them are the seasoned hikers, striding steadily upwards, hardly breaking a sweat, boots caked with a patina of dust from Snowdonia, the Mournes, the Jura, the Dolomites.

"Not far to go now!" we shout, encouraging the discouraged, full of energy now we are heading down. "It's worth it when you get up!"

Tired, we stumble occasionally on loose rock. The sun, still strong late in the afternoon, saps our energy. We glug water greedily, gallons of the stuff. As we round a corner in the path, the lochan comes into view, glimmering invitingly in the sun. Getting closer, we hear cries and screams. Some brave souls are swimming in the freezing mountain water, washing away their fatigue from a long day's hike, splashing water into the air that descends in rainbow fronds back to earth.

Lower and lower, we enter the bracken fronds and scrub that line the gorge. Here the midges prepare to strafe and bombard. These wee beasties, afraid of sun and wind and rain, lie in wait in this sheltered spot. Hikers jump and cry out, whisking at faces and bare skin, trying to keep them off. The midges gather in clouds above people's heads, eager for a good feed. We speed up, not wanting to be dinner for the nibbling insects.

In the distance, at the bottom of the valley we can see the hostel. Hungry bellies rumble, knowing that a big feed is waiting for us. The last mile or so, we are running on empty but walking on air. Fellow hikers are full of smiles and congratulations. We share stories and tips and slap each other on the back. What a day!

The sun dips below the valley edge as we arrive at our journey's end. We turn and look up at the mountain top, now bathed in a stunning golden glow. An eagle passes overhead, majestic and deadly. We embrace in silence, stunned by the beauty and proud of our achievement, already full of plans for the next challenge.

10: Writing Checklist

As you read, check how many of the recommendations below are followed by the description. Then, use the checklist to help you write your own.

Remember that these are *recommendations* from an experienced teacher, not *requirements*. Allow them to help and guide you, but don't allow them to restrict you; if you have a different idea and feel confident and excited about it, then give it a go!

- [ ] Create an emotional 'journey'.
- [ ] Structure by passing of time and/or by shifts in focus.
- [ ] Describe time of year and day.
- [ ] Describe weather.
- [ ] Describe colours.
- [ ] Describe sounds.
- [ ] Describe tastes, smells and touch sensations.
- [ ] Describe people.
- [ ] Describe/suggest their emotions.
- [ ] Use a small amount of direct speech.
- [ ] Use symbolism.
- [ ] Zoom in to tiny details.
- [ ] Zoom out to bird's-eye view.
- [ ] Speed pace up/slow pace down.
- [ ] Freeze time.
- [ ] Use present tense.
- [ ] Describe the past of the scene.
- [ ] Describe the future of the scene.
- [ ] Use imagery, simile, metaphor, personification.
- [ ] Use paragraphs and sentences of varied length.
- [ ] Use accurate spelling, punctuation and grammar.
- [ ] Write c450-c750 words.

11: A description of a crowded street

You are advised to spend the correct amount of time on this section (check Appendix 1 for your exam board's time).
Write in full sentences.
You are reminded of the need to plan your answer.
You should leave enough time to check your work at the end.

You are going to enter a creative writing competition.

Your entry will be judged by a panel of people of your own age.

Describe what you see, hear and feel in a very crowded street.

11: The Description

We stand by the park at the south end of the street, waiting for the green man. Sparrows flit and flutter in the bushes. A tram swooshes past while in the bandstand the Garda Band play jaunty brass versions of old songs. The crowd, a mixture of tourists and office workers on their lunch break, claps at the end of each tune. The traffic halts and the green man flashes. We step across the road and plunge into the pounding heart of the fair city.

The street is narrow, and we are funnelled into a dense crowd of shoppers and tourists, buskers and pavement artists, delivery cyclists and security guards. The city cacophony reaches high above us, up beyond the Georgian facades, and out into the narrow strip of sky above us. Visitors from a quiet faraway village, we are exhilarated and intimated in equal measure by such movement and noise and colour. We pass on along the cobbles, gazing in wonder at this river of life. So many streams of consciousness gathered like threads by a master weaver, are merged into this vibrant tapestry of life in the big city.

A mime artist walks into an invisible wall, an acrobat tumbles and cartwheels across the street, dancers leap and bound, seeming to float above the cobbles. An accordion wheezes and splutters, music in compound time skipping and diving through the air. A circle of admirers stops to listen, feet tapping, jigs and reels. The voice of a lone singer reaches us, the words in the old language, a slow mournful song.

We pause for refreshment and respite at a coffee house which seems to open out endlessly behind its street frontage, like a Tardis, room after room, level upon level, spiral staircases rising and falling. A cup of sharp Arabica in hand, we stand on the balcony to see the street from above. It is an everyday miracle seen from up here; the throng is like the never-ending flow of particles in a physics experiment, darting and surging, turning and pulsing, never colliding, always ever onwards. Our hearts beat faster. The beat of the city, the rhythm of life.

We keep going. Not far now to the river. Great business deals are being struck in the shops along the thoroughfare. Silver crosses palms and there is money to be made. Everything is available, from a pin to an elephant: engraved shillelaghs, Aran jumpers, illuminations from the Book of Kells, apples, oranges, pears and chocolate, GAA jerseys, black pudding, Modernist literary masterpieces, brogues, tailored suits, brack and tea.

Laden with bags, we reach the end of our journey. The crowd thins now as people go in separate directions, off home to suburbs and dormitory towns, tower blocks and cottages. We stand for a moment by the running river. A brave swimmer sweeps past beneath us, carried by the powerful ebb of the tide. We breathe in and peace returns to our bodies. The shock of the city, the jolt to the senses, is exciting, dramatic but almost too much for those of us used to life at a slower pace.

We head for the railway station and home, whistling a jig and looking forward to the next visit to the big city.

11: Writing Checklist

As you read, check how many of the recommendations below are followed by the description. Then, use the checklist to help you write your own.

Remember that these are *recommendations* from an experienced teacher, not *requirements*. Allow them to help and guide you, but don't allow them to restrict you; if you have a different idea and feel confident and excited about it, then give it a go!

- [ ] Create an emotional 'journey'.
- [ ] Structure by passing of time and/or by shifts in focus.
- [ ] Describe time of year and day.
- [ ] Describe weather.
- [ ] Describe colours.
- [ ] Describe sounds.
- [ ] Describe tastes, smells and touch sensations.
- [ ] Describe people.
- [ ] Describe/suggest their emotions.
- [ ] Use a small amount of direct speech.
- [ ] Use symbolism.
- [ ] Zoom in to tiny details.
- [ ] Zoom out to bird's-eye view.
- [ ] Speed pace up/slow pace down.
- [ ] Freeze time.
- [ ] Use present tense.
- [ ] Describe the past of the scene.
- [ ] Describe the future of the scene.
- [ ] Use imagery, simile, metaphor, personification.
- [ ] Use paragraphs and sentences of varied length.
- [ ] Use accurate spelling, punctuation and grammar.
- [ ] Write c450-c750 words.

12: A description of a factory

You are advised to spend the correct amount of time on this section (check Appendix 1 for your exam board's time).
Write in full sentences.
You are reminded of the need to plan your answer.
You should leave enough time to check your work at the end.

You are going to enter a creative writing competition.

Your entry will be judged by a panel of people of your own age.

Write a description with the title, 'The factory'.

12: The Description

It sits, huge, squat and unloved, deep in the heart of the county, under a leaden winter sky. Chimneys and antennae reach up from the surrounding mud, warning lights blinking mysteriously. A line of pylons marches across the horizon bringing the vast gulps of energy consumed by the ravenous factory. A concrete causeway through the mud sees round-the-clock traffic as lorries come and go, laden with goods. Hanging in the air is a strange, familiar smell, a flavour really, sickly and overpowering: chocolate.

The dawn shift don hairnets and overalls and head to the factory floor. As the doors open, the smell becomes intense: sugar and cocoa, peppermint and orange. The operatives move swiftly to their stations, experienced and skilled. They are ready. The production line shudders into action. Chocolate arrives, warm and slick, pumped through pipes from the mixing room. The fluid drips and flows into moulds, filled with precise squirts from a row of nozzles. In a moment, they are gone, into the chiller which travels the full length of the factory.

The duty manager whizzes to the other end of the line on a folding bike. Each mould is grabbed from the chiller as it emerges and smashed onto the packing table. Thousands of chocolate coins made every minute, packed into golden nets in a moment and then sent for delivery. It is August and the Christmas chocolate production is already in full flow.

The manager does a quality check, making sure the outline of the queen's face is crisp and visible. She wonders, as she often does, how it would feel to have all these coins for real. Real gold, pounds sterling. She pops one in her mouth – tasting the product is an important part of quality control. She nods, satisfied with this batch.

On the walnut whip production line, there are raised voices. One of the people tasked with placing the walnuts onto the top of the chocolate cones keeps missing.

"They move too fast!"

The duty manager shifts him onto another line. Walnut whips wait for no man. She takes his place for a while just to get the line up to speed again, eager to meet today's production target.

Time passes slowly under the fluorescent lights but finally the morning tea break arrives. The workers head for the canteen, removing hairnets, masks and overalls and becoming individuals again. Buttered toast, sausage sandwiches and bowls of porridge are doled out liberally by the canteen staff, who also keep the workers topped up with vast mugs of tea and coffee, strong and sweet. No chocolate though. Never chocolate.

Down in the loading bay, a lorry backs into the dock. Forklift drivers work swiftly, twirling steering wheels and squeezing levers with inch-perfect dexterity, loading the HGV in record time. Meanwhile, a sugar tanker arrives, with sugar fresh from the fields. It is an eye-watering amount of the stuff, fine white sucrose, running like water, glittering with flavour.

A child, eyes open with amazement, watches all the toing and froing as he waits in line at the factory shop. He hopes to be served by Willy Wonka himself but apparently he's not on shift today. Not to worry. He heads off home with a bag of chocolate and a smile.

Back inside the factory, the lines keep moving, always moving. Nozzles rising and falling, chocolate ever flowing. Sugar and milk and cocoa and theobromine. Food of the gods.

12: Writing Checklist

As you read, check how many of the recommendations below are followed by the description. Then, use the checklist to help you write your own.

Remember that these are *recommendations* from an experienced teacher, not *requirements*. Allow them to help and guide you, but don't allow them to restrict you; if you have a different idea and feel confident and excited about it, then give it a go!

- ☐ Create an emotional 'journey'.
- ☐ Structure by passing of time and/or by shifts in focus.
- ☐ Describe time of year and day.
- ☐ Describe weather.
- ☐ Describe colours.
- ☐ Describe sounds.
- ☐ Describe tastes, smells and touch sensations.
- ☐ Describe people.
- ☐ Describe/suggest their emotions.
- ☐ Use a small amount of direct speech.
- ☐ Use symbolism.
- ☐ Zoom in to tiny details.
- ☐ Zoom out to bird's-eye view.
- ☐ Speed pace up/slow pace down.
- ☐ Freeze time.
- ☐ Use present tense.
- ☐ Describe the past of the scene.
- ☐ Describe the future of the scene.
- ☐ Use imagery, simile, metaphor, personification.
- ☐ Use paragraphs and sentences of varied length.
- ☐ Use accurate spelling, punctuation and grammar.
- ☐ Write c450-c750 words.

Appendix 1: Exam Board Information

The below information is correct as of summer 2023. However, please check carefully with your exam provider as exam boards make regular changes to exam timings, marks allocations, weightings, syllabus codes etc.

Exam Board	Paper/Section	Time Allowed	Marks (%)
AQA (8700)	Paper 1 Section B (8700/1)	45 mins	40 marks (25%)
Edexcel GCSE (1EN0)	Paper 1 Section B (1EN0/01)	45 mins	40 marks (25%)
OCR (J351)	Component 02 Section B (J351/02)	60 mins	40 marks (25%)
WJEC Eduqas	Component 1 Section B	45 mins	40 marks (25%)

Appendix 2: What the examiners are looking for

GCSE Exam boards will assess your writing against two Assessment Objectives:

AO5	Communicate clearly, effectively and imaginatively, selecting and adapting tone, style and register for different forms, purposes and audiences. Organise information and ideas, using structural and grammatical features to support coherence and cohesion of texts.
AO6	Candidates must use a range of vocabulary and sentence structures for clarity, purpose and effect, with accurate spelling and punctuation.

This exam board language, however, can feel a bit vague. After all, what does "coherence and cohesion" mean? Who decides what is "effective" and what isn't?

It is possible to answer those questions:

- Coherence means that your text should make sense as a whole, meaning the reader should understand clearly what's going on.
- Cohesion means your sentences should follow the normal rules of Standard English written grammar.
- It is your examiner, ultimately, who will decide what is effective and what isn't.

However, rather than answering these questions theoretically and hypothetically, the descriptions in this book aim to show in practical terms how it's possible to give your examiner what they are looking for, within the time constraints of the exam, whilst also showing off the full range of your creativity and writing technique.

What makes the descriptions in this book excellent exam answers?

The twelve descriptions in this book show how you can make good decisions about tone, style and register in order to write a text in the required form: a description. The descriptions interweave varied language technique, well-crafted text structure and expressive description to create effective and imaginative texts that examiners would reward with high marks.

The descriptions also showcase accurate spelling, consistent punctuation, clear grammar and varied sentence structures.

Moreover, these descriptions are short – no more than 750 words. The first drafts were written under the same conditions as the ones you will face and therefore reflect what is possible in such a short time.

Printed in Great Britain
by Amazon